Even the Angels Must Laugh

• • • • AGAIN • • • •

Jan S. Doward

Edited by Jerry D. Thomas
Designed by Michelle C. Petz
Cover and inside art by Thomas Dunbebin

Copyright ©1998 by
Pacific Press® Publishing Association
Printed in the United States of America
All Rights Reserved

ISBN 0-8163-1408-X

98 99 00 01 02 • 5 4 3 2 1

Contents

Introduction to Unexpected Humor

Somehow, it never seemed to me that for all his wisdom, Solomon caught the full significance of an out-of-sync time for laughter. In his famous comment about the seasonal things of life, he simply stated there's "a time to laugh." But it's a lot more hilarious when it's not time. It always seems funnier when humor comes at right angles to a solemn, worshipful situation.

I think I first came to this realization after choking and crying as I desperately tried to suppress my laughter during a church service several years ago. It happened in a small country church—one of those compressed sanctuaries in which the pulpit and pews fit tightly together, not so much for good eye contact, but merely to crowd in more people. It was a hot summer day, and all the windows stood open for the sorely needed cross ventilation. The staid Scandinavians who made up the bulk of the congregation sat impassively listening to their favorite old-time lay preacher intoning some sure and comfortable theology.

In the midst of his sermon, Mr. Swanson sagely asked a rhetorical question. I can't recall what he actually queried, but I distinctly do remember that as, if in answer, a cow mooed right on cue. The bovine sound effects came through the open window behind the pulpit.

This set me up. I put my hand to my mouth, but more was to follow. Swanson, hard of hearing as he was, only leaned forward in the pulpit and cupped his ear.

"How's that again, brother?" he asked seriously.

I couldn't hold it! Grabbing my handkerchief, I stuffed it in my mouth. My wife nudged me. But it was no use. I knew she had better control and would somehow save her laughter for later when she could have a good belly laugh at home. Not me. I suffered intense gagging and tears. My head grew hot, and I sensed my face was red from the effort of holding in check the happy sounds I wanted so much to make. What made it worse was the fact that all the saints sat soberly looking straight ahead, sedately listening as if nothing had ever happened.

Since that time I've been on the lookout for others who have experienced similar moments, moments when laughter has irreverently elbowed its way into worship. I've asked evangelists, pastors, and church-goers in general all over the country to share with me. Laughter knows no denomina-tional barriers, but I have always hastened to add in my quest that I definitely do believe in reverence. It's just that I have a sneaking hunch even the angels sometimes must bend over in laughter over the unexpected.

The Hazards of Baptism

My friends and family know I'm always on the prowl for true, unpublished stories. One day my youngest daughter phoned.

"Dad," she laughed, "you'd have cracked up today in our church. During a baptism, one of the older ladies lost her wig! The pastor picked it up like some drowned rat and handed it to her as she stepped out of the water. We had to sing about two dozen hymns before she'd come out to meet the congregation. It was too funny!"

I imagined it was! Baptisms, I've discovered, have a special built-in mechanism for potential humor.

I can only visualize what I would have suffered had I been attending the little Southern Baptist church in back-country Georgia during a morning they had scheduled a husband-and-wife immersion.

From what I was told, it was one of those cozy arrangements in which the deacons have to move the pulpit and lift the floorboards to expose the baptistry. Sheets were hung over wires to form a "dressing room" on each side of the baptismal tank. The husband had already been baptized and returned to change into his clothes, when his overweight wife descended the rickety stairs to the water. But the last step cracked and collapsed on her. As she lunged forward, staggering past the pastor, her arms wildly thrashed about for something to grasp. She caught the sheet on the opposite side and tore it down, exposing her shocked husband to the whole congregation. As he stood there in the buff, he made a quick and stunning decision. Diving headfirst into the baptistry, he disappeared from sight.

I can only imagine how many hymns they had to sing to bring the congregation back into line after that performance!

• • • • •

Uninvited persons in the baptistry are unusual. But when it does happen, the ceremony takes on new meaning.

With the pulpit moved to one side and the floorboards lifted, this particular church's fairly wide platform was much narrower. But the old gentleman slated to offer the benediction chose to remain in his seat on the rostrum during the baptism anyway. At least he intended to remain in his seat!

With so many being baptized that day, the elder grew weary of his straight-back position and began leaning his chair against the wall. As time passed, he started teetering the chair slightly. But once, the teeter wasn't slight enough. In a flash he was up-ended. With legs extended upward and hands frantically grasping for invisible handles, he went fully clothed into the baptistry.

For those in the congregation who had temporarily glanced away, it seemed like a fantastic disappearing act!

• • • • • •

> The first rule for rural church baptisms is to notify all participants when the floorboards are removed. The second is to maintain composure at all costs if they aren't.

One little deaconess, whose sole job was to supply towels to both curtained-off "dressing rooms," began her duties in earnest as she passed back and forth with armloads of towels. But between one of her passes across the front, when her back was turned, the deacons lifted the floorboards!

Without a glance, the deaconess turned and headed back the way she had come. But this time, her path led straight into the water. She didn't resort to water-walking, and she didn't scream or back away. She went right on in without so much as a flicker

on her firm facial expression. Resolutely wading across the baptistry, she never lost stride. Still holding the towels high, she climbed the steps on the opposite side and continued her duties as if nothing had happened. It would be hard to match that for total composure!

• • • • •

> Somehow those rural churches with the hidden baptistry beneath the rostrum never seem to lend themselves to the sanctity of a baptism. At least the preliminaries can certainly be distracting.

During one morning service, I watched in dismay as the deacons grunted and strained to slide the pulpit to one side and lift the floorboards. The clouds of steam that rose from the baptistry led one of the deacons to lean over to test the water.

"Ouch!" His loud cry shattered the sanctuary. Before the congregation could recover from that outburst, he grabbed a huge paddle from the adjoining room and began stirring the water vigorously.

From that moment on, my mind kept fighting to focus on reverence instead of conjuring up all sorts of scenarios of a blistered minister and lobster-red candidates emerging from the baptistry one by one.

• • • • •

But small country churches certainly don't have a corner on potentially humorous situations. Let me share something that happened recently in a plush suburban setting. This church had installed a glassed-in section in the lower part of the baptistry so that the congregation could witness the underwater activity during immersion.

Apparently, bubbles and bloated faces are more meaningful for many folk, adding a special dimension to the sacred rite. But this time, the whole congregation was afforded far more visual excitement than was originally scheduled.

The first man baptized arose from the water totally confused and headed up the stairs to the ladies' dressing room. By the time he realized his mistake, another candidate had taken his place in the water. He patiently waited behind the curtain for the right moment. Just as the next party slipped under, he went into action. But the audience never saw the baptism. Their wondering eyes beheld only a black-robed body desperately swimming underwater across the baptistry!

• • • • • •

> Communication is absolutely vital for any baptism. The candidates must understand what to expect or they can conceivably take all sorts of poses, postures, and appearances before the plunge. The problem is compounded when there is a language barrier.

One Russian couple presented themselves for the ceremony in a very dignified church. He could understand a little English, but his wife could not grasp one word.

She entered the baptistry first and immediately held her hands in front of her, palms together, poised as if about ready to take a dive.

"Will someone please go get this lady's husband so he can tell her what to do," the minister pleaded.

Suddenly called from the men's dressing room to go interpret, the anxious husband rushed out onto the rostrum clad only in his long johns.

That otherwise conservative congregation had a most difficult time suppressing their amusement. After all, how often did they witness that sort of display during church?

•　•　•　•　•

Every minister has his own preference for baptismal attire. Some wear weighted robes while others prefer old suits that obviously keep on shrinking. But I heard the story of one preacher who preferred hip boots. Since he was a short man, those fishing waders gave him a rather compressed look—as if somehow, his head and shoulders had been jammed into his legs. But the appeal of wearing those waders held him firmly. They held him even firmer during one evangelistic tent meeting.

A portable tank was placed near the front of the tent, but the attendant responsible for placing the false bottom in the tank forgot his duty. When the hip boot evangelist climbed into the tank he sank clear to his chin. With the waders filled to the brim, he was literally riveted in place.

"Would someone please pull the curtains and get me out of here!" he cried.

Imagine the effect on the waiting audience after that sort of introduction to the baptismal ceremony!

• • • • •

Shortly after a successful Vacation Bible School, a Kentucky Baptist church scheduled a baptism, mainly for children. As one little fellow stepped into the baptistry, he found himself up to his chin in water. Overwhelmed by the depth, he immediately began dog-paddling across the glassed-in baptistry—much to the amusement of the congregation. He tried to turn back when he reached the pastor, but then decided to swim to the other side. Instantly, the pastor's arm shot out like a shepherd's crook and pulled him back.

"If I can catch them, I can baptize them!" the pastor quipped to the audience.

The little boy just beamed with delight as the entire congregation roared with laughter.

• • • • •

Due to a large number of candidates preparing for baptism, a well-known evangelist decided to use a local swimming pool instead of a church baptistry. One of the many candidates lined up at the shallow end of the pool that day was a heavy-set woman who secretly held a very morbid fear of being immersed. It was one thing for her to talk about the rite in the dry setting of some church but quite another when the moment arrived in the pool. The very thought of having her head and upper torso under water was too much. Suddenly she startled everyone, including the evangelist, by raising both her hands above her head and pleading in a loud voice.

"Oh, save me from the water! Oh, save me from the water!"

To say that the occasion was a memorable one would be a vast understatement. For the evangelist to secure her hands, then get her entire body immersed and lifted upward without being pulled clear under himself in the struggle was a major accomplishment that few who witnessed it will ever forget.

• • • • •

Shall we gather at the river? Yes, indeed! Nature has a way of enhancing the beauty of baptism. But it also has a way of totally shattering the sanctity of the rite, causing wild thrashing and splashing at the most inopportune moments. Smoothness of operation depends on water temperature and the clearness of the stream or lake. Blue lips and chattering teeth are only one aspect of the inherent dangers. The prospects of either the candidate or the officiating minister suddenly disappearing down some hidden hole always lurk as a distinct possibility. And the danger of these natural hazardous possibilities is often in direct proportion to the size of the person being baptized.

As one very obese lady presented herself for a river baptism, the deacons whispered their concern to the minister. Since she tipped in close to 300 pounds, they would certainly be willing to assist the pastor in both the lowering and lifting.

"Oh, I believe I can handle this without any problem," the pastor graciously smiled. "Once in the water her weight will not be much of a factor."

He was SO wrong! As he dipped her under the water, the sheer weight of her huge frame yanked him off his feet. He too plunged beneath the dark depths. About fifteen feet downstream, the pastor surfaced, arms waving as he gulped for air. The chunky candidate had apparently settled on the muddy bottom. Fortunately, the deacons were right on hand to follow the tell-tale bubbles and hastily waded to her rescue.

Many songs were sung before order was restored among the congregation lining the shore. Perhaps a little prayer session helped too!

• • • • •

Church Bloopers

Spoonerisms are such great blessings because they allow the whole audience to laugh spontaneously without fear of frowns. The accidental transpositions of sound always seem funnier when said at some large assembly. Maybe it's because there are more people laughing and it takes longer to settle everyone down.

At a great ecclesiastical gathering in the Midwest a few years ago, the keynote

23

address speaker began with . . . "Here we stand, puke and weany men that we are . . . I mean weak and puny men . . ."

It is doubtful anyone remembered much of anything else that evening.

• • • • •

The tongue can do marvelous things even with simple messages. One person who was given the assignment of announcing the hymn number became rattled once his tongue got tangled on the initial effort.

"We will now sing nymn humber . . . I mean hum nymber, er, er . . . num hymber . . . Oh, just sing 175!" he finally blurted out. It was probably a good thing that the organ could help drown out most of the snorts and snickers once 175 was under way.

• • • • •

A spoonerism is funny enough when a speaker recognizes it and attempts to correct it. But when he or she continues without the slightest hint as to why everyone is so highly amused, it adds a special touch that creates even more humor.

One minister who had gained a reputation for his slips of the lip attempted to generate enthusiasm at a youth song service and happily exclaimed, "It's such a beautiful day today I think we ought to have a sitting fong!"

Whatever fitting song was selected came laced with grinning amusement that kept a perplexed look on the puzzled pastor's face as he led the group in singing. This look, in turn, kept the youth hanging happily onto his every word in keen anticipation of another possible blooper. That pastor may never know what he said that kept his listeners so riveted to his message!

•　•　•　•　•

A simple word or phrase blunder can be just as devastating as any spoonerism. One Baptist preacher, while waxing eloquent in his closing remarks exclaimed earnestly, "Now if you can get that into your heads, then you'll have it in a nutshell!"

Few, of course, ever remembered much of the sermon but most would never forget the ending.

•　•　•　•　•

A popular TV preacher, noted for his dignified demeanor and articulate delivery on camera, once had to make a quick recovery from a slip during an out-of-studio meeting. In an effort to show his audience the connection between several Bible verses he said in his typical cathedral voice, "Now let me give you a co-text (which sounded like Kotex). I mean companion text."

• • • • •

Every business organization, government agency, and scholastic discipline has its own in-house terminologies which are totally meaningless to the general public. The various denominations are no exception.

One evening a Seventh-day Adventist evangelist got carried away with his personal background in church work. Without explaining the exact meaning of the church's organizational structure, he proclaimed with a flourish, "I was a Union officer at one time."

Puzzled, a little sixth-grade girl leaned over and whispered to a friend of mine, "I didn't think he was old enough to be in the Civil War."

• • • • •

One of the most classic bloopers on file occurred in a Christian college testimonial meeting. A tearful freshman concluded his personal testimony with a memorable request.

"Please pray I'll not be found sleeping with the five foolish virgins when Jesus comes," he sobbed.

The student body has long since scattered, but whenever any of them chance to meet, a simple mention of that moment still brings howls of laughter.

• • • • •

Announcements can always hold their own when it comes to blunders. And they often go uncorrected, which leaves the audience in a state of bewilderment and curiosity.

Prior to the eleven o'clock service, a Mrs. Hand requested the pastor to remember her ill husband during the morning prayer. The good man agreed but when the time came, he went to the pulpit and informed his waiting flock of a very serious matter.

"Sister Husband would like the congregation to pray for her hand."

• • • • •

> Sometimes the introduction of a guest speaker can get so sticky that it is the better part of wisdom to let it go and allow the visiting preacher the honor of any correction.

He was supposed to be introduced as Pastor Brazee; but when the announcer came to his part, he smiled and said in gracious tones, "We are happy to have with us this morning. Pastor Brassiere."

I've always been glad I didn't do it or I'd have had to leave the rostrum very quickly on an emergency call!

• • • • •

> Nervousness before a large audience is often the cause of some verbal mistake.

During one jammed Seventh-day Adventist camp meeting there were over 20,000 people present. On the platform was a church official named Elder Belleau (pronounced Bellow), who was slated to offer the morning prayer. But the nervous ministerial intern, whose only job for the occasion was to introduce the church leader, got up before that great concourse of people and solemnly announced, "Elder Pray will now bellow."

It took more than thirty minutes of singing to bring that congregation back to some semblance of prayful attitude. Each time it seemed the proper moment had arrived, a ripple of laughter would begin somewhere, and off they'd all go again. Truly a great moment to remember!

• • • • •

Getting carried away with the sweep of some great concept often can lead to marvelous wording and confusion.

I once attended a meeting in which the enthusiastic preacher requested all those old-timers, born before the turn of the century, to stand. Since his sermon was on last-day prophecies, he hoped to emphasize how these folks had actually seen many things fulfilled.

It took a little effort but one by one over the audience the white-haired ones managed to struggle to their feet. The preacher then meant to say, "You have seen many prophecies fulfilled," and then politely ask them to be seated. But instead, his mind leaped forward anticipating his next point, and in a loud voice he grandly proclaimed, "YOU HAVE BEEN SEATED!"

The dear old saints blinked in stunned confusion. Slowly, however, it dawned on them that the preacher, caught up in his own grandiose oratory, was continuing without further need of their participation and they gradually slipped into their seats.

Fortunately for me, enough commotion was created to cover my own amused sound effects.

Exciting Evangelism

Some evangelists have a real knack for the highly dramatic and sensational. But this can lead to goofs, which do far more than enhance the quality of any meeting.

One evangelist I know felt it was imperative to illustrate eternal fire. His visual aid was designed to awaken even the most lethargic. Placing about a quarter inch of gasoline in the bottom of an old-fashioned washtub he struck a match at the appropriate time.

Whoosh!

"Eternal fire" burst forth, sending dark smoke to blacken the newly painted church ceiling. Somewhere behind the ominous fury of flames and smoke, the evangelist desperately tried to make his point in spite of the commotion of the fire and apprehensive audience. It seems that he had never practiced this performance because two deacons leaped to their feet and quickly carried "eternal fire" outside the church.

The audience never forgot the visual aid even if they couldn't remember what it was supposed to illustrate. But I've often wondered what the neighbors thought as they witnessed that washtub ablaze in the churchyard. It was certainly an exciting way to attract attention—but not necessarily to the preaching service.

•　•　•　•　•

> Unexpected audience participation always holds immeasurable possibilities of added thrills not on the evangelistic program.

One evangelist, caught up in the sensational arts, decided that the most effective method to establish the sureness of Daniel's prophecy that Europe would never be united was to bring back former world leaders from the "grave" and have them give their "testimony" over the PA system. On cue, his assistant backstage was to speak into a microphone placed on the bottom of a bucket to give the voice that eerie tomb-like resonance. But the assistant didn't get very far into his act before things got out of hand.

"I am Napoleon," he said slowly. "I am speaking from the grave tonight . . . I tried to unite . . ."

"EEEEYOW!" a woman on the front row screamed. Throwing her hands heavenward, she slipped out of her seat and slumped to the floor in a dead faint.

Since medical assistance was necessary, all eyes were riveted on the activity up front and the evangelist never could get his momentum back.

• • • • •

> When any evangelist hankers to use an illustration borrowed out of biblical times he had better use the real thing. Substitutes can cause embarrassment.

One very demonstrative young preacher decided to reenact that moment when the prophet Jeremiah broke the "earthen bottle" as a symbol of how Israel would be broken in his day. Instead of using a clay jar as the prophet did, the evangelist tried to smash an old-fashioned glass milk bottle.

"As this bottle is shattered so was ancient Israel!" he proclaimed with finality.

But when he vigorously threw the bottle to the floor, it happily bounced back and came to a rest atop the piano. While it was fortunate for those on the front row that it didn't break, it now stood serenely perched on the piano and no amount of enthusiastic audio report of how Israel was shattered could counteract the reality of that visual aid quietly resting right before everyone's eyes.

• • • • •

For sheer visual excitement, it would be hard to match the efforts of one Southern California evangelist. He attempted to depict the dream of Daniel 2 where the stone struck the great image and shattered it. Timing, however, is absolutely essential in pulling off any creative visual aids. Miscues are disastrous. His was disastrous!

The evangelist had rigged up a wire running from high in the balcony clear to the theater stage where he had placed a large plywood break-away image all painted according to the biblical description: head of gold, chest of silver, belly of brass, legs of iron, and feet of iron and clay. A pulley was secured on a wire from which hung a large, weighted papier-mâché "stone" several feet in diameter.

A local church volunteer was to station himself way up in the balcony and release the "stone" on cue for the grand climax.

"Now when you hear me read that text from Daniel 2:34 'a stone was cut out without hands, which smote the image upon his feet that were of iron and clay, and brake them to pieces,' you release the 'stone' down the wire. OK?"

The old man nodded. It was simple. Hear the text and release the "stone." Nothing to it.

On opening night the theater was filled. The magic of the moment swept the evangelist up in an ecclesiastical euphoria. Suddenly breaking from his usual format, he decided to open his Bible and dramatically read the whole section of Scripture as an introduction. Without thinking of the consequences, he inadvertently read verse 34 and kept right on reading.

The man in the balcony sat up with a start. The text! Since that was his cue, he immediately let fly the "stone" which vaulted over the heads of the audience to its target. The evangelist looked up just in time to see the "stone" heading right for the image. Holding out his hand like some cop trying to stop traffic he shouted.

"Not NOW, brother! NOT NOW!"

But it was too late. The "stone" struck the

image, sending the break-away parts in all directions just as it was scheduled to do for the finale.

For those on the evangelistic team, it must have been a howler. For those in the audience not familiar with the specifics of Bible prophecy, it must have been a startling experience.

• • • • •

Most evangelists roam the platform. With their penchant for prancing and pacing, few remain behind the pulpit very long. I've only seen one who stayed very close to the pulpit and he was a man with a very dry throat. Placing four glasses of water on the pulpit, he accomplished one of the most marvelous physical feats I have ever seen— he grabbed each of those four glasses in turn and swallowed the water they contained without the slightest cough, choke, or pause in his sermon.

• • • • •

Most speakers drift, however. And thanks to the cordless microphone, they can roam to their heart's content without getting tangled in some trailing cord. But one evangelist I know got far more action than he ever anticipated.

For his subject of Bible prophecy from Revelation, three giant-sized plywood angels were strung on wires. Each was to be sent flying through the "midst of heaven" by an off-stage assistant. With an appropriately-timed yank on a pulley, the assistant could send the "angels" flying one after another in a sort of three-layered angelic pattern. It was impressive, to say the least.

It became even more impressive one evening when the assistant accidentally sent all three flying at once. The evangelist who expected to speak at some length on the meaning of each separate "angel" suddenly found himself doing a lot of fancy dancing while ducking and dodging as those "angels" flew, one after another. That evening's clever choreography was really extra special because few would ever see again such unrehearsed gyrations accompanied by some of the fastest moving spotlights on record.

• • • • •

Sleeping during religious services has always carried inherent humor. A variety of these actual sleeping occurrences have filtered through to me over the years, including cases where those responsible for closing the service suddenly awoke from slumber, abruptly jerked to a standing position and with raised hands, prematurely asked the congregation to "rise for the benediction."

But the one I like best happened right in the audience during a large evangelistic tent meeting in Southern California several years ago. Without any of the typical snoring, an old man quietly snoozed on the front row, totally oblivious to his surroundings. But while he slept, a fuse blew, plunging the audience into darkness. Only the public address system remained on. The evangelist never lost a beat.

"So long as you can still hear my voice, I'll keep right on preaching," he explained. "My attendants will get the lights fixed shortly."

He wasn't far along in his "dark" discourse when the old man awoke. Hearing the preacher's voice, but seeing nothing aroused all his dormant energies.

"Oh, pray for me! I've gone blind!" he shouted loudly.

Two teen-age girls seated behind the old man got so tickled at the sudden interruption that they quickly dropped to the ground and crawled under the tent wall to laugh it off outside. I'm afraid if I had been there, I'd have had to join them.

• • • • •

Public address systems often amplify far more than singing or sermons, though. An evangelist friend of mine consistently wears a cordless mike during his meetings. Once, however, he forgot to turn it off when he recessed to the men's room during the song service. Interspersed throughout the singing, sounds could distinctly be heard in the auditorium—the sound of whistling, of the urinal flushing, of the washbasin filling, and of paper towels pulled from the holder and crumpled.

When my friend returned to the platform, he whispered to one of his associates, "How's it been going?"

The associate pointed toward the lapel mike and whispered back, "You ought to know; you were on!"

More Than Music

Music is supposed to be as much a part of worship as prayer and preaching. Yet for all of its possibilities, it can become the source of some highly entertaining episodes.

A local church orchestra conductor made the mistake of inviting me to play my trumpet with his musical group. It is true I once tooted the trumpet in a high school band, but since those distant, hazy days I have only played for my own amazement and amusement. But at the time, I felt relatively sure I could handle most well-known hymns without too much difficulty. I always felt that if I could hum the tune, then with a little practice I could play the hymn. The problem was I can't ever remember practicing together.

On the opening performance during church service, the orchestra seemed to struggle through the first hymn. The blending of the instruments never did come off right. It sounded a bit wheezy and off-key, sort of like a New Year's celebration at times. At best, the trumpet is not a subdued instrument and during the first rendition I could easily be heard above the woodwinds or whatever else happened to be there that morning.

Then the conductor made a startling announcement.

"We will now play the hymn right across the page, number 398."

"Hymn 398!" I gulped. "I just played that!"

The orchestra sounded so much better on the next piece.

• • • • •

Through the years, I have had a part in creating just enough musical disasters to avoid filling out any questionnaires for latent church talent. Memories that range from playing the wrong piece to shouting "Stop! Stop!" when I ran out of breath during a congregational sing-a-long with my trumpet have etched deeply into my mind the need for staying musically incognito.

Knowing this, my youngest daughter and her husband once tried to trick me into joining a newly forming church orchestra. When the questionnaire was distributed I discreetly passed mine on without so much as blinking. But unbeknown to me, they took one and filled in my name, address, and phone number, and printed "Trumpet" on the instrument line. Then came the clincher.

"When would it be the best time for you to practice?" the questionnaire asked.

They filled in: "I don't need to practice!"

They only confessed to this diabolical scheme when the call to join never came.

Obviously, I was far and away too talented for any local church orchestra.

•   •   •   •   •

Caution should always be the watchword for purchasing so-called musical bargains. One church to which I belonged several years ago rushed into buying a used organ simply because a musically inclined minister transferring to a new location wanted to unload his personal instrument. He admittedly purchased the organ originally from a skating rink and that should have warned the unwary congregation. But they were taken with the notion of getting such a large-size organ for such a whale of a discount. The sales pitch was tremendous and even backed by a recital that seemed to captivate most folk. Yet the recital never brought out the fullest extent of the organ's possibilities. That was left for a guest organist several weeks after the purchase was finalized.

Everything went smoothly during the worship service until the conclusion of the morning prayer. While the congregation was still on its knees, the organist—intending to provide the special meditative-mood music—accidentally activated the wrong buttons. Wafting over the sanctuary was the distinct sound of trap drums, tambourines, castanets, and cymbals in a sort of syncopated beat that was very noticeable with the Bach-type music we had been hearing.

I wish now that I had peeked because I am sure the guest organist must have been frantically fumbling with all the stops and buttons or whatever other gadgetry was on the panels. But once triggered, the only way to stop the jazzy percussion section would be to hit the off switch or pull the plug. But that, of course, would have made the muffled snorts and snickers passing through the congregation seem even louder.

• • • • •

Organ preludes, interludes, and postludes are traditionally designed for reverence. The temptation, however, to use this convenient musical cover to carry on a conversation is too much for some.

One organist glanced down in disgust at two ladies near the front row who were caught up in very animated whispering. Determined to grab their attention and lift their souls to more sacred matters, he increased the volume. Utterly oblivious to their surroundings and what had happened, the women only raised their voices accordingly. Square-jawed and determined not to be outdone, the organist stepped up the volume even further. The organ swelled to a great crescendo, yet the women vigorously pursued their conversation.

By the width of their mouths and the lively gesturing, the organist suspected they had resorted to shouting. In total abandonment, he grimly departed from the musical score and jammed everything to a halt leaving the women's loud conversation suspended for all to hear. In the sudden silence of the sanctuary, the startled congregation heard a most vociferous but fascinating culinary remark.

"BUT I FRY MINE IN LARD!"

Music can be such a blessing when rightly used!

• • • • •

> Unrestricted volunteering of musical talents can pose problems of unusual dimensions. To have singers, for instance, suddenly decide to share their unscheduled talent is rare, but when it does happen, few in the congregation ever forget it.

The minister of a large college campus church was well into his sermon when a woman far up in the balcony decided it was time for her to share her singing ability. Leaving her seat, she made her way downstairs and into the main sanctuary. Striding with determination right up to the rostrum, she informed the startled minister of her intent.

"I want to sing!" she declared.

The time for special music had long since passed, but the poor preacher—not knowing what else to do—stepped aside and allowed the eager singer to use the pulpit for her a cappella rendition. When she finished, the minister went right on with his sermon, but in the back of his mind was a determination to secure church board action to curtail any future spontaneous performances.

• • • • •

Fortunately, she at least sang a religious song. The congregation in a small northwest country church, however, was not so lucky. An elderly member suddenly became inspired to sing, but to the astonishment of everyone that Sabbath morning he shared, "Down by the Old Mill Stream"!

Regardless of whatever else was heard that day none could erase the memory of listening to those words of the old love song, "You were sixteen, my village queen, down by the old mill stream!" What this had to do with worship remains a mystery to this day.

• • • • •

What musicians wear often makes more of an impression than their music. I cannot remember one piece a student organist played that morning in the college chapel but I distinctly do recall seeing her reaching for the foot pedals in her pajamas!

She had obviously overslept and had rushed from the women's dorm clad only in her coat and pjs. Thinking nobody would notice anything unusual, she had played with total abandonment, displaying her enormous talents. The organ, however, was located in the balcony and all those seated at a certain angle below could look up and behold legs draped in silky bright pink.

I suppose with a little creative selectivity, certain hymns and gospel tunes could have been used to accompany this sort of appearance.

•　•　•　•　•

Proper dress is so important to musicians that any discrepancy just prior to a performance can cause sheer panic. Several years ago, a choir director discovered his pants sadly sagging in the rear moments before a sacred concert. He had lost both buttons that held his suspenders! One of the astute local townsfolk, however, volunteered to meet the emergency by supplying him with an old-fashioned horse blanket pin. The director's trousers held firmly enough but every time he lifted his arms while conducting, his coat would part in the back exposing that giant-sized safety pin.

A few fervent "Amens" would have helped to cover the continued audience amusement.

• • • • •

In the days when choir directors waved batons and women wore their hair in buns, a certain dignity and solemnity pervaded performances. But musical numbers could get positively dramatic.

One director let his baton slip during a lively hymn and it sailed like a dart to its target—the organist's hair. It struck with such force that it remained in her bun during the rest of the rendition. Whatever exciting selection was being sung that day could have been enhanced with a special stirring arrangement of that old gospel song, "The Fight Is On!"

• • • • •

> Singing from memory always has inherent hazards. The human mind is quite capable of going totally blank even with familiar words.

While singing "The Lord's Prayer" during a wedding, a friend of mine succumbed to a lapse of memory as he approached the finale. To the dismay of the pianist accompanying him, he repeated—like some broken record—"For Thine is the kingdom . . . is the kingdom . . . is the kingdom . . ." Such recycling while groping for the right words would certainly awaken even those dreamy-eyed patrons and relatives who never seem to listen much during a wedding.

• • • • •

> Hunger and boredom often drive people to do the strangest things. Musicians are no exceptions, especially if they are youthful.

One teenage choir member, feeling the Sunday morning service was dragging too

much, began thinking of his stomach. This activated his memory of a bag of potato chips in his car. Since he sat where the audience was not fully visible, he slipped from his seat and inexorably began crawling to the nearest exit. Once outside, he ran to the parking lot, retrieved the bag of chips and hastily returned. Placing the bag between his teeth he dropped to his knees and ever so carefully pushed open the door. While concentrating on the carpet ahead of him so as not to make a sound, he inched his way on all fours to find his choir seat.

Suddenly the whole congregation stirred. Glancing up, he discovered to his horror that he had accidently taken the wrong door and was midway out on the platform!

It is very doubtful that any musical selection could have erased that sight in the minds of the congregation. At least, none was found that Sunday morning.

• • • • •

> Selecting the wrong door has always been loaded with definite but distinctive possibilities for disaster.

In the days when men wore collar buttons, one young choir member lost his just prior to a religious college performance. With everyone else nearly ready, he frantically searched all over the dressing room but to no avail. Finally in desperation, he burst into what he thought was the men's room to ask for help. "Do any of you happen to have an extra collar button?" he loudly pleaded. But to his dismay, he had opened the wrong door and was standing in full view of the audience clad only in his shirt and shorts.

The ensuing laughter prevented him from making his appearance for the first number of the sacred concert even though he had found a button stud at the last moment.

Sneaking in later to blend with the rest of the choir took a certain amount of finesse, of course.

• • • • •

One singer I know sat near the front of the church and prepared to share his talents with the congregation. His wife and two-year-old daughter were sitting in the same pew. That is to say, his daughter was standing in the pew next to him, so she could be as tall as he was.

Then the girl had a wonderful sharing idea. Taking the bright red ribbons out of her own hair, she neatly stuck them into her daddy's thick curly hair.

Not feeling the touch of her tiny fingers, the singer stood up for his song with both ribbons showing nicely. For him, the constant smiles spread across the congregation during his solo were a great mystery. Not until he sat down did he learn of those bright red decorations in his hair!

People may have forgotten the song he sang that day, but they will never be able to erase the mental image of those visual aids in the singer's hair!

● ● ● ● ●

Those Embarrassing Moments

When it comes to embarrassing moments in church, I personally have achieved my share. In fact, I can easily identify with those who have reason to blush.

Once I enthusiastically taught a Bible class which was delightfully spellbound and smiling throughout my entire arm-waving teaching. I was almost inclined to believe I had achieved the level of a master teacher until I later discovered the cleaner's tag conspicuously stapled to my sleeve!

• • • • •

I've even walked right into a church sanctuary with red suspenders dangling down my sides. I would have made it clear to the front of my waiting class except that my dear wife luckily spotted me first. Her whispered concern over my absent-mindedness sent me back-peddling to the nearest men's room where I solemnly vowed never to wear suspender's again. Then and there I pledged conversion to a belt!

• • • • •

Belts may seem superior to suspenders, but they aren't always a sure thing for support either. Not if you're terribly overweight anyway. One of the most mortifying experiences on record happened to a very heavy-set preacher before a youth audience. He wanted to show the young people that the gospel was really like a life preserver and intended to wear one around his waist at the height of his sermon on salvation.

The problem was he couldn't find a genuine preserver but had to settle for a brightly colored, child's plastic inflatable ring. He pulled this out from behind the pulpit at the appropriate time, and while blowing it up paused to pant out the great spiritual lesson. Then slipping the plastic ring over his head and shoulders, he wiggled it down to his chest. As he maneuvered it further down to his waistline, the ring fit so tightly that he was forced to squirm and twist to get it into place.

Finally in desperation, he inhaled as much as possible and pushed the ring down. At that precise moment, his pants fell off! Obviously he could not see over his tummy, and with all the bodily contortions and the snug fit, he was totally unaware of what had happened. The unexpected roaring laughter of the entire student body did alert him that something was dreadfully amiss, but this only created a puzzled expression on his face which punctuated his predicament and generated still more laughter.

One can only imagine the added hilarity

when he tried to take a step with his trousers tangled around his ankles and that inflated ring around his waist. Ah, what tremendous truths can be taught with such simple devices!

• • • • •

Skirt fasteners can be just as hazardous as any belt though. While reaching for a high note, one singer discovered that reality. Her skirt fastener, unable to bear the strain, let loose. Her skirt settled in a heap on the floor. Fortunately, she had chosen to stand behind the organ that morning. After completing her musical number in her slip, she stooped over, gathered up her skirt and discreetly exited through the door directly behind her.

Only the men on the rostrum witnessed the performance, and one wonders if they had as much composure as the lady singer.

• • • • •

No one could ever fault an elderly southern lay preacher for his thorough Bible preparations but sometimes his personal appearance seemed in need of improvement. Once while he was seated on the rostrum awaiting the time to preach, a deacon whispered to him, "Your shirt tail is hanging out."

The old gentleman nodded a thank you and while looking straight ahead proceeded to tuck in the exposed tail of his shirt. The problem, however, was that he tucked in more than what he was wearing. When he got up to speak he pulled down the American flag!

•   •   •   •   •

At another service this same elderly gentleman got a message about his appearance.

"Your fly is open," the deacon seated next to him whispered.

Sure enough. So with a quick, discreet zip the old preacher closed the embarrassing gap. But in so doing he inadvertently caught the end of his necktie. When it was time to speak, he tried to get up but found himself frozen in a sitting position, unable to straighten.

• • • • •

> Pastors are supposed to be trained in the fine art of friendly greetings. The warm handshake, the shoulder or arm squeeze, the pat on the back and smiling face are all part of the well-disciplined schooling to make folk feel welcomed in church. But while pressing the flesh has a long-standing tradition of success, head-patting has its special perils.

One dignified associate minister of a large city Christian church took his cue to greet the elderly ladies gathered in the church lounge Sunday morning. As he approached one dear old saint on the sofa, he smiled broadly.

"Well, good morning, Mary," he said, bending over to gently pat her on her head. But as he walked away the buttons on his coat sleeve somehow caught her wig and he walked off with it attached. Neither Mary nor the minister were aware of what had happened. She sat there smiling in the bald, still pleased with the little head blessing but unconscious of why all the other ladies were laughing so much.

"What's so funny?" she asked.

But none could stop laughing long enough to tell her.

Meanwhile, one of the deacons caught the minister down the corridor and asked him a profound question before he entered the sanctuary.

"Just what is that wig doing on your sleeve?"

Returning the wig and explaining the whole situation to dear Mary required a great deal of diplomacy. It's doubtful any young buck fresh out of the seminary would come equipped to handle that sort of problem. But then, head-patting probably wasn't on any of the school's curriculum anyway and the gesture might never occur to a ministerial intern, however gifted.

• • • • •

Children on the loose in church can create more havoc and embarrassment in less time than just about any single thing known to man. Parents, parishioners, and preachers alike cringe when some child escapes to unknown parts in the sanctuary during the worship service.

How well I remember being startled beyond my wits when a toddler who had crawled from the rear of the room suddenly emerged from under the pew directly in front of me while I was preaching. It was one of those tight little country sanctuaries and the effect was dramatic.

I quickly leaned over the pulpit and pointed downward.

"Whose is it?" I blurted out.

Then another question pressed for an answer as I fumbled with my notes: Where was I?

• • • • •

Easter Sunday is traditionally associated with the solemn dignity of a very special service. But back at the turn of the century, the congregation of a large Baptist church in Michigan was totally stunned by the results of one active three-year-old on the prowl—

her plan: to pick a bouquet of pansies from a lady's bonnet.

At best, little Lucile was never known for her quiet behavior during church services. Her wealthy father had lavished gifts on the church right down to the beautiful stained glass windows. But his little daughter gave also. Her impromptu acts and speeches during Sunday services provided embarrassment not only for her entire family but the whole congregation as well.

On that particular Easter Sunday, she made a promise though.

"I'll be good."

Her parents doubted that but Father held her on his lap, where for a little while, she seemed content. Her snappy eyes darted around the congregation searching with intensity for some fresh idea. Finally, she spied a woman wearing a bonnet filled with what looked like pansies. Back in those days, designers didn't garnish women's headgear with a few imitation flowers but often placed a mini-garden aloft. Lucile's little hands itched to pick those pansies. "Me sit on the floor," she whispered to her father. Thinking she was weary of his lap, he allowed her to slip from his grasp.

Instantly, Lucile began crawling under the pew, crossed the aisle, and positioned herself directly behind the woman with the big Easter bonnet. At first, she tried picking her bouquet gently but when none came loose, she gave the flowers a big yank. Not only did the whole bonnet come off but the wig securely pinned to it came also, exposing a shiny bald head.

In a high-pitched voice that could easily be heard clear to the back row of the balcony, Lucile yelled "Mama! Mama! Come quick! I've scalped her!"

But Lucile's piercing voice was instantly followed by another only slightly lower in tone. Grabbing her head in her hands, the woman let fly a volley of profanity that sent shudders throughout the horrified congregation. While the oaths were still fresh on her lips, she churned in a flurry of fast footwork down the aisle and out of the church never to return. She even left town without a forwarding address!

One can only visualize the minister later

standing by the church door after the service with a frozen door-to-door salesman smile pasted on his face. Picture the parishioners passing by and—between stifled laughs—shaking his hand and telling him how nice his Easter sermon was. The truth was, all any of them would ever honestly remember was the scalping episode.

• • • • •

> Unfortunately, children never seem to plan their escapes at a time when the congregation is standing to sing. If somehow they could cue their exploratory trips to such times, it would provide a nice cover for parents to pursue with some semblance of dignity and without disturbing too many people.

I'm sure a friend of mine certainly wished his little son had held off for a long six-stanza hymn. Jimmy slipped loose one morning in a large religious gathering. The challenge of negotiating through that forest of legs intrigued Jimmy, and off he scooted

for the front row. His father followed up the aisle in a half-crouch position peering down each row and wistfully calling, "Jimmy . . . Jimmy!"

But Jimmy was long gone. I could measure his progress by the way people jerked to attention as he passed below them. Women especially seemed vulnerable, emitting little frightened squeaks as they half leaped to their feet when Jimmy grabbed their legs as he worked through the unusual obstacle course.

My poor miserable friend finally retrieved his small son way up front near the rostrum. The long trek back with Jimmy in tow was an agonizing experience. It is doubtful he remembered who spoke that day or even the special music. I know I can't!

• • • • •

> Children are not the only ones who can cause embarrassment in church. It can range through every age, depending on the personality, perception, or functioning faculties.

One day a devoted son-in-law graciously consented to take his dear wife's elderly mother to church. Since she was hard of hearing, he carefully escorted the ninety-year-old lady down the aisle to the section where earphones were attached to the back of the pews. Once she was seated and the earphones adjusted, everything seemed ready for worship. But the timing was off. Right then the minister requested that the congregation bow their heads for a moment of silent prayer. Everyone obeyed except this elderly soul who cocked her head and frowned. Then in her own penetrating voice she shattered the sanctity of the meditation.

"I can't hear a thing!" she exclaimed loudly.

No, indeed!

• • • • •

> Stray pets on the loose in church can cause a variety of exciting events which may or may not blend well with the worship service.

A stunned Methodist minister suddenly became very red-faced one Sunday morning when his friendly collie ambled in from the next door parish. The pastor might have adapted this into some appropriate illustration of a warning about leaving gates and side doors open, or even the positive aspects of living in balmy California, but the sermon was not in progress at that juncture. Instead, a large number of the congregation were quietly kneeling at the Communion rail; and the dog, seeing all those beautiful, shining countenances at his level, tail-wagged happily down the line, licking faces as he went.

Regardless of the minister's embarrassment, how warm and touching can a Communion get anyway?

• • • • •

What began as an enlightening vespers designed to show the close relationship between health and spirituality turned into a tense and embarrassing verbal shoot-out which prompted me hastily to close the meeting.

I had arranged with a physician who specializes in this topic to speak, then open the floor for discussion. It was during the latter part of this period that an oversized woman stood to her feet.

"You spoke about obesity tonight but my doctor tells me that I have glandular problems and have to be obese."

Tightening his grip on the platform microphone, the doctor said firmly, "There were NO obese people in the concentration camps!"

The large lady shot back, "I demand an apology!"

"And I'm not giving one!" the doctor snapped.

Everything happened so rapidly I hardly had time to sort matters out, but I quickly suggested we stand for the closing hymn. Fortunately, I had pre-chosen a peaceful one, because under the pressure I could have inadvertently gone to the listing of hymns for "special occasions" and taken the old rallying one, "Sound the Battle Cry"!

● ● ● ● ●

Few visiting church dignitaries ever have the attention of monkeys as well as people at a worship service, but a church leader from the U.S. preaching in southern India certainly did.

In an open-air meeting, the primates were chattering and swinging from limb to limb in the nearby trees of a grove while the speaker urged the local congregation to be active in missionary work among their own families and villages. In the middle of his sermon, he asked a rhetorical question:

"Who will go to spread the gospel?"

To drive his point home, he repeated, "Who? Who? Who?"

Suddenly the monkeys in the trees came alive. In unison, they echoed back, "Whooo . . . whooo . . . whooo!"

And who among that crowd of people could help but respond after that performance?

• • • • •

For all the advertisements extolling the virtues and advantages of adhesives for false teeth, those who wear them know the embarrassment of possible looseness and the sound effects of clatter.

One elderly preacher never seemed to find the right "stickum" and his sermons were invariably punctuated with a distinctive clicking and clacking sound. One morning, however, he lost his teeth altogether! At the height of his sermon, they flew right out of his mouth! Still, he may have been old, but he was quick. With a quick wide-open jaw, he instantly caught his escaping teeth

midair and went right on preaching.

Those who witnessed this fine reactionary performance almost wished for an instant slow motion replay to see just how he actually snapped those teeth back in place so quickly.

• • • • •

When a white preacher is to be a guest at a black church, the chances of committing some public "faux pas" increases tremendously.

A friend of mine desperately wanted to make a good impression in his opening remarks. The only thing he could think of off-hand was the fact that the ushers and usherettes were dressed sharply in white, including white gloves.

"Everyone looks so nice this morning," he said as he smiled at the black congregation. "White is my favorite color!"

It's always much safer to stick with well-prepared notes.

• • • • •

A visiting white speaker I know brought an

entire black congregation into gales of laughter one morning all because of a cultural misunderstanding.

After the sermon, the black pastor sitting next to him leaned over and whispered, "Open the doors of the church."

Now that expression is not a familiar one to most white folk. The guest preacher never linked opening the doors of the church with an altar call.

Raising his eyebrows, the guest speaker whispered incredulously, "You mean that?" The black pastor nodded.

Without further prodding, the white preacher left his seat during the closing hymn and resolutely walked to the rear of the church to open all of the doors. A deacon standing back there caught the significance of what had happened and suggested to the guest speaker that he not return to the rostrum. But instead the preacher squared his shoulders and stalked back down the aisle. As the closing hymn ended, he stepped to the pulpit mike to make his announcement.

"The doors of this church are now

officially opened!" he declared emphatically.

The congregation came unhinged with laughter leaving the white preacher confused and rapidly glowing red.

• • • • •

> Carefully listening to directions is so important, yet when pressed for time, the brain can easily short-circuit causing a variety of delicate situations.

One guest speaker, already a bit late for his appointment, asked a deacon directions to the men's room.

"Downstairs," he pointed. "Second door on the right."

The visiting preacher thanked the deacon and hurried below knowing he had only a few minutes before he was expected to join the local church leaders in the minister's study prior to going onto the rostrum.

Doors? The downstairs hallway seemed a maze of them. But at that moment the guest preacher had other priorities. The fine distinctions of choosing the proper door didn't register nor did he even bother to read the sign as he took the first door on the right. It only took a glance to see that he had entered the wrong rest room, but the sound of the door opening behind him drove him at top speed into one of the stalls. He just sat there with his legs hoisted high for fear that the woman might see his trousers.

More women came. Some even began rattling the stall door to hurry whoever was on the other side. Since there was only one other facility, it didn't take long for the traffic to back up. Soon the ladies' rest room was jammed with irate females who were becoming increasingly distressed over the delaying party in the first stall. It was bad enough hearing all the muttering and cutting comments without being so cramped that his legs seemed about to collapse and fall to the floor.

The guest speaker scarcely breathed for fear that one of the younger set might crawl underneath or peek over the top and reveal the stark truth. Precious minutes fleeted away until finally, after sweating it out about as long as he thought he could endure, the rest room eventually was empty again.

Those waiting for him in the minister's study simply could not imagine what was detaining him since he had been seen talking to the deacon in the foyer earlier. Finally when he did show up, he offered no explanation for the delay.

After all, why add further embarrassment with a detailed description of the shattering experience?

• • • • •

Fortunately for the young ministerial intern, the Adventist camp meeting congregation would never be privy to his plight in the men's room. It happened during camp pitch time a few days before the great gathering . The rest rooms were all being refurbished and he, not noticing the "wet paint" sign, sat down and was promptly stuck with a new type of highly adhesive paint. At first he thought he could wiggle free but soon it became apparent he was glued to the toilet seat. His cries for help were finally heard and several of the other interns arrived to unbolt the seat that still remained attached to him. Draping a blanket over his back to hide the embarrassing attachment, they drove him in a pickup truck to the local Adventist doctor.

When the good doctor unveiled the problem he couldn't keep from laughing.

"I've seen a lot of these, he said, "but I've never seen one framed before!"

• • • • •

In spite of repeated Scriptural revelation, it is difficult to imagine the impact of a resurrection from the dead. Yet one Sunday morning near the turn of the century while my grandfather was preaching, he and all his parishioners momentarily may have conceived they witnessed one right before their very eyes.

Back in those days funerals were often held in churches and the funeral paraphernalia sometimes remained in the vestibule behind great folding doors that led to the main sanctuary.

My dad and his brother Al discovered a

casket on rollers that Sunday morning and decided to have some fun rather than listen to their father preach. Dad suggested Al climb aboard the casket and he would push him around for a nice ride. Now as far back as I can remember, Uncle Al was huge. In school, the boys were known as Big Doward and Little Doward. It always seemed to me that Dad had more wit than weight. So that bright Sunday morning Al snuggled down in the silk-lined casket while his little brother wheeled him around making figure eights and all sorts of exciting maneuvers only a preacher's son could imagine. Al sat there grinning from ear to ear. But suddenly my dear Dad had a tremendous burst of inspiration. Why not send Al down the main aisle?

Before Al could change his mind and climb out, Dad quickly flung open the center folding doors and shoved the casket as hard as he could. I never learned what Grandfather's subject was that morning. Hopefully it was something appropriate because as Al sat bolt upright in that casket, he sailed directly down the aisle and struck the pulpit with such force that it startled all the dear saints.

Later that same Sunday, Grandfather did a little laying on of hands, and not in ordination either!

Yet as I have reflected on what happened, I've wondered if any spirited evangelist has ever thought of that idea for a live illustration.

•　•　•　•　•

Toilet paper ads invariably make their pitch

in favor of tissue softness. You seldom hear anything about the strength of the paper or its ability to withstand violent tugs and strains. Yet it is this very ability that permitted my father to make his unique appearance with the rest of the deacons prior to Communion service that memorable Sunday morning.

Dad had tried to coordinate his urgent visit to the men's room with the weekly entrance of the deacons to serve Communion. Since he was last in the two dozen deacon line-up, it seemed simple enough. There would be time for him to hurry up from the basement stairs and get in line with his partner in the narthex.

It was always such an impressive and dignified ceremonial entrance. The great pipe organ would fill the cavernous church with some pompous tunes while the deacons would march two by two down the long sloping aisle to the rostrum and peel off to flank the ornate Communion table with a dozen deacons on each side.

The organ started to play that morning as the deacons straightened their coats and ties and squared their shoulders preparatory for the grand entrance, when one of them glanced over at Dad at the last moment.

"Doward, what's that trailing behind you?" he whispered.

Somehow the toilet paper had hooked on Dad's suspender buttons and remained intact as he headed for the line-up. Yards and yards of the strong paper came off the roll. Nothing broke.

He had a line running all the way from the narthex to the men's room in the basement where still a remnant of the roll remained.

At that time, I was glad his deacon colleague had spotted the trouble and saved so much embarrassment. But years later, I've often wondered about the effect if Dad had made it all the way to the front. It certainly would have been a Communion service few would ever forget.

•   •   •   •   •

Old fashioned churches with belfries have always held a special appeal. The sound of a church bell ringing clear on a Sabbath morning holds a charm that evokes the very essence of poetry. But the person on the inside—assigned to the pulling of the rope—can turn the occasion into an embarrassing bit of personal prose.

In a church where I attended, a diminutive deacon energetically pulled so hard one Sabbath morning that the heavy bell swung clear over. Rather than let go his grip, he clung tenaciously to the end of the rope and was yanked clear to the ceiling. The folk in the lobby who witnessed this fascinating zipping-to-the-top then dropping-to-the-floor episode had a most difficult time entering the sanctuary with a straight face.

•   •   •   •   •

Postscript

The toughest test of self-control during those moments of unexpected humor occurs when everyone is watching.

I was asked to be the guest speaker at a statewide religious meeting in Iowa a few years ago. The meeting took place in a high school auditorium where the stage backdrop composed of long, colored burlap strips hung from the ceiling. It actually did resemble solid paneling.

Just as I was introduced, I happened to glance toward the left-hand wing. At that precise moment, a stage attendant tried to lean against what he thought was the wall. He flopped clear out of sight. All I could see were two feet sticking out from under the burlap. It was like a typical Hollywood sight gag.

Suddenly I was on! Nobody in the audience saw the accident except those in the balcony to my far right, and they were in stitches, which didn't help me a bit. Just glancing toward them almost triggered spasms of laughter from me. What to do? I adjusted my notes and then spied the grain of wood on the podium. Oh, how I studied that wood! Concentrate! Every ounce of my energy was momentarily diverted to that wood!

Later when I could reflect on the occasion it occurred to me to make a slight personal adjustment to Solomon's wise words. "When it's not time to laugh but it's funny anyway, concentrate on something else." Sometimes it's the only way out.

A few years after this little book was first published I received a long-distance call from a very upset lady who thought I had transgressed by relating any humor that happened in church.

"I'm sorry you feel this way, but these were all stories I have collected through the years. None were made-up, I did not relate any contrived humor or tell jokes, " I explained.

She still was not satisfied, so I continued. "Well, just what would you do if some unexpected funny thing happened during a religious service?"

"I might smile, " she answered firmly, "but I wouldn't laugh."

I felt extremely sorry for the woman. "You know," I said, "we were made for laughter, not for tears. Tears came after the entrance of sin."

That seemed to help a bit and we parted in at least a somewhat state of good will. I really hope she thought about God's gracious gift of pure, unadulterated laughter.

"It was so funny, I almost split in half trying not to laugh out loud in church!"

Have these stories reminded you of things you've seen? If you've witnessed a hilarious incident in church, write it down and send it in! We're collecting stories for a possible second book like *Even the Angels Must Laugh Again*. If you have a story to share, send it to:

Angels Must Laugh Editor
Pacific Press
PO Box 5353
Nampa, ID 83653

Or send it by e-mail to:
jertho@pacificpress.com

While we cannot acknowledge receipt of your story, each person submitting a story that is used in the book will receive a free copy of the book when it is published.

Share your laughter . . . and your love for your church family!

WELCOME TO
Kite Day

Today is Kite Day.

1

Dave and Jean made their own kites.

Dave's kite is beautiful. Jean's kite is plain.

The kites soar up into the deep blue sky.
They dip and dive in the wind.

Then a strong gust breaks Dave's kite in half.
"Oh no!" Dave cries. The tail of his kite drifts
to the ground.

Jean's kite flies higher and higher,
like a sturdy brown bird.
Finally, she reels it in.

"Next time, let's make a kite together,"
Jean tells Dave.

"Okay," says Dave. "Our kite will be strong *and* beautiful."

8